Cherokee Connections

An introduction to

genealogical sources

pertaining to

Cherokee ancestors

Myra Vanderpool Gormley, CG

GENEALOGICAL PUBLISHING Co., Inc.

Reprinted by arrangement with the author
by Genealogical Publishing Co., Inc.
1001 N. Calvert St., Baltimore, MD 21202
1998, 1999
Library of Congress Catalogue Card Number 98-72718
International Standard Book Number 0-8063-1579-2
Made in the United States of America

To my sister,
Mary Jo Vanderpool Grant,
who continually encourages
me to pursue
our Cherokee connections

Cover: Drawing of a Cherokee woman by Beverly Gilbert Bills from her *Parade of Historic Fashions Coloring Book* for the Mary Ball Chapter, National Society of Daughters of American Revolution, with her kind permission. A typical dress worn by Cherokee women about the time of the Trail of Tears (1838/39) was the *tear dress*. Because of the scarcity of scissors, the material was torn and then sewn in straight seams. The dresses were made of cotton and brightly decorated, often with ribbon. The ornateness of decoration distinguished the everyday dress from the Sunday dress.

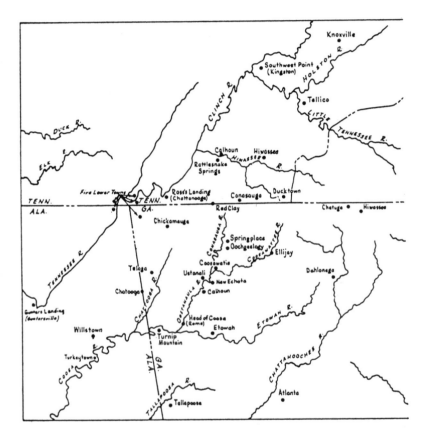

Cherokee towns and settlements in the federal period, 1785–1838.

From *The Cherokees*, by Grace Steele Woodward. Copyright (C) 1963 by the University of Oklahoma Press.

Contents

Maps ... iv, vi, viii, 48

Preface ... vii

1. Family legends ... 1

2. A mini-history ... 13

3. Sources and records ... 26

4. Select bibliography ... 49

5. Repositories ... 52

6. Cherokee publication sources ... 53

7. Index ... 54

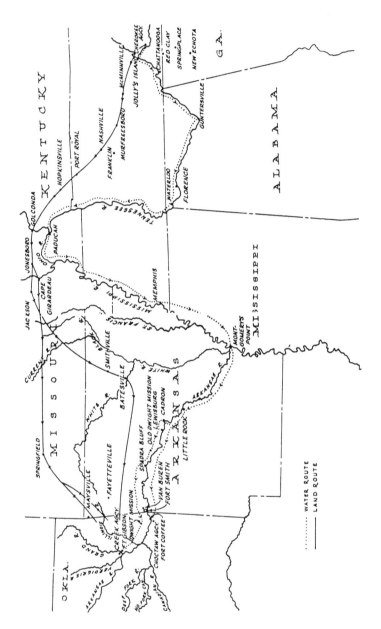

Routes taken by the Cherokees during their removal to the west, 1838–39.
From *The Cherokees*, by Grace Steele Woodward. Copyright (C) 1963 by the
University of Oklahoma Press.

Preface

During the past decade I have fielded many questions pertaining to Cherokee research from my newspaper column readers and from Prodigy[R] Genealogy Bulletin Board users. As a result I have heard many family stories and been privy to numerous genealogists' research adventures. My own family passed along its treasured legends pertaining to alleged Cherokee ancestry—in several different lines, and it seemed peculiar to me that so many families have identical oral histories relating to Cherokee heritage.

Like many genealogists before me, I decided to find out if there was any truth to my family's stories so I bravely waded into the records of the Five Civilized Tribes. I soon discovered that I was not fully prepared for the enormity and complexity of them. Nor was my historical background adequate, even though as a native of northeastern Oklahoma I had been exposed to more than the average amount of Cherokee history. I went in search of more information in order to comprehend the historical and genealogical records pertaining to Cherokees. It has been my good fortune to have many knowledgeable friends and colleagues who shared their expertise and guided me along the way. I also have the world's best sister who has been my head cheerleader, but who refuses to allow any family legends to go without historical challenge.

It is my hope that this book will help you in your search for your Cherokee heritage, and perhaps my experiences can make your research somewhat easier and less costly. I would like to thank especially Wally Waits, Marybelle Chase, Jerri Chasteen, Gloria Murray, Dorothy Tincup Mauldin, Johni Cerny, Laura McCoy Herbert, Julie Case, Clare Midgley, Linda Edelstein, Joanie Utley Brink, Rhonda McClure, and the kind staffs at Muskogee, Oklahoma Public Library, Oklahoma State Archives, Oklahoma Historical Society, Family History Library, National Archives—Southwest branch at Fort Worth and Suzzallo Library of the University of Washington.

Myra Vanderpool Gormley

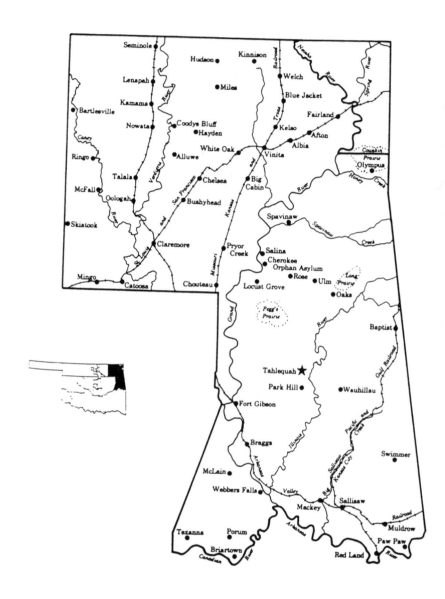

Cherokee Nation: Important Places
From *Historical Atlas of Oklahoma,* Third Edition, by John W. Morris, Charles
R. Goins, and Edwin C. McReynolds. Copyright (C) 1965, 1976, 1986 by the
University of Oklahoma Press

Family legends

Have heard all your life that somewhere back in the family tree is a Cherokee ancestor? If so, you are not alone. This is a recurring story told in many American families, and many of us are seeking to prove such connections.

The staff at the Fort Worth branch of the National Archives receives thousands of letters from researchers who are trying to prove that they have a Native American ancestor—usually a Cherokee. And, librarians and professional genealogists across the country confirm the numerous inquiries pertaining to requests for Cherokee genealogical research. This legend ranks among the Top Three in popularity, which includes the *Three Brothers Came to America* and *Black Dutch* tales that are told in American families. However, a Cherokee line may be easier to trace than the other two.

While some family stories can be proven, they seldom turn out exactly as the oral history was transmitted. Be forewarned that the pursuit of your Cherokee connections may lead you into a labyrinth that seems to have no end. But do not let that stop you from trying to prove your heritage. For regardless of the end results of this research adventure, the search for Cherokee ancestry is one of the most fascinating genealogical quests into the pages of American history that you will ever experience.

Getting started

However, before you tackle Cherokee lines, if you are new to genealogical research, prepare by tracing some of your other ancestors first. The experience gained in finding and using basic genealogical records will prove invaluable later. Also, learning your way around various repositories is highly recommended prior to taking the plunge into the almost overwhelming amount of material and records that you will encounter during your search for Cherokee ancestors.

If the family legend handed down to you simply claims that your great-great-(whatever)-grandmother (or grandfather) was

Cherokee or part-Cherokee, you must first trace, generation by generation, the family line connected to her or him. Naturally, if you try to skip generations, you will miss the link. Since few Cherokee records of any genealogical value exist prior to 1800, if your alleged Cherokee connection is earlier than this, it may be impossible to prove—with acceptable genealogical evidence. But you will never know unless you search. So do not make assumptions about what you may or may not find in any records. The only way to know is to search. But, because of the tediousness and time-consuming type of research involved, you probably will have to do a great deal of this research yourself as it can be too expensive for the average family historian's budget. Probably the best way to solve this problem is to spread the expense over several years. Consider it a long-term project, because it probably will be.

Basics first

One initial difficulty pertaining to this research is accepting the fact that the basic genealogical research must be done, and it must be done first. There is a tendency to want to jump back to the time of the Trail of Tears (1838), or even earlier, and start looking for Cherokee ancestors in those time frames I have never known anyone who has been able to do this successfully. Do first things first.

■ Where (state) did your families live at the time of the 1920, 1910 and 1900 federal censuses? If you don't have this information, make it a high priority project.

■ Are your families all listed as *white* in these enumerations? If so, then you have your work cut out for you. But, don't be discouraged, the adventure has just begun.

It is in these census records that you may encounter the first conflicting information about your ancestors. They may not be living where you thought they were, and other discrepancies may appear, plus they may not be enumerated as "Indians."

Like all genealogical research, you need a foundation on which to build. Start with yourself. Write down everything you have heard about your ancestors—especially the Cherokees connections.

- Talk to your relatives—separately. Record the information they give you, then compare their stories (privately, of course). Determine if the stories could be true—historically. You can verify many dates and localities by checking federal census records and United States, state and local histories. Keep in mind that family legends have a way of getting entangled and sometimes attributed to the wrong side of the family. For example, your maternal grandmother may have claimed that her great-grandmother was part Cherokee. Do you know which of her four great-grandmothers she meant? And, since it is unlikely that anyone ever asked her, you are going to have to determine who each of these women were and trace them all in search of the Cherokee connection.

- Where (county/state) did your purported Cherokee ancestors reside, marry and/or die, and when? If you do not have this information, make it a research goal.

- As you talk to your relatives focus on obtaining **names**— especially **maiden names** of your female ancestors— **places** and **dates.** You can not conduct any genealogical research without a name, a date or time period (even approximate ones will do) and place (locality). Without this basic information you are looking for a needle in the haystack and will become discouraged before your research has really begun. Some of your family members may provide information that is obviously incorrect, but don't argue with them or contradict them. Let them talk. You can verify data later, but get the stories while you can.

Name problems

Names are always a problem in genealogical research, but they are a frequent and major problem encountered in Cherokee research. For example, in the records you may find your ancestor listed under two different names—one being his Cherokee name, the other an English one. Also, there is great temptation on the part of eager genealogists to consult various compiled lists of Cherokees, such as the *Cherokee Emigration Rolls, 1817–1835,* too soon in their research and therein discover such names as *The Squirrel, Otter Lifter,* and *Chu-ne-quat-ees-kee* and be frustrated because at that point it may be impossible to recognize ancestors under their Cherokee or translated names. Some Cherokees changed their names, for various reasons, so allow for this possibility. Most researchers will have only a surname to work with in the beginning. And for a mixed-blood Cherokee ancestor, it likely will be a Scot, Irish or German surname.

Be careful about accepting family legends that claim your Cherokee's name was something fanciful such as *Little Flower* or warrior-sounding, such as *Brave Eagle.* Cherokee names usually did not translate that way. You are far more likely to find *Big Belly, Bark Waterlizzard, Deer Biter, Stinking Fish* or *Wrinkle But* [sic] in your tree.

The search for Cherokee ancestors must adhere to the same research principles as any other type of genealogical work. Start with the known and work backward to the unknown, carefully linking each generation. Not all of our Native American ancestors were Cherokee, so keep an open mind to the possibility that your Indian blood may come from another tribe.

Degree of blood

Most researchers are surprised to discover their supposed full-blood Cherokee ancestor turns out to be one-quarter blood or less. If some of your ancestors are enumerated as Indians in the 1900 census, and appear in the special schedules therein, pay close attention to the information listed about the tribe and quantum of blood. The former probably will be correct, but the latter may not be. The reason being that minor children and *restricted Indians* (generally those of more than one-half degree Indian blood) were subject to having their financial affairs regulated by government agents. Therefore, many sought to avoid these controls by *understating* their degree of blood. And, you may discover the information given on this census will not match the information on your Cherokee ancestors listed on the Dawes or Guion Miller rolls. As in all records, there are discrepancies.

Prior to the passage of the Curtis Act in 1898, which provided for the preparation of tribal rolls, making of allotments by the Dawes Commission and dissolvement of the tribes' governments, neither the Cherokees nor any of the Five Civilized Tribes indicated the quantum of Indian blood of its members on their rolls. Every member of the Cherokee tribe was entitled to equal rights, so there had been no reason to keep track of degrees of blood. Of course, there had always been distinction between the full-bloods and mixed-bloods, but this manifest itself in intra-tribal political controversies, not in tribal rights.

Different tribes

Problems arose when the Dawes Commission became involved, particularly in instances where the applicant's parents were members of different tribes. The commission determined the degree of blood based on the mother's tribe. Thus the child of a full-blood Choctaw father and a full-blood Cherokee mother was enrolled as one-half Cherokee by blood, even though he or she was 100 percent Native American. In cases of mixed black and Indian parents, the commission enrolled them as a freedman with a zero degree of Indian blood. Many of these freedmen later tried unsuccessfully to be moved to the *by blood* roll, which would have given them more land.

Filtering facts from fiction

You may not be aware of it, but there are many identical or very similar stories told about Cherokee ancestry, and they appear so frequently in our families that a family historian must examine these folk tales and legends closely and honestly. There may be some truth in them, but they probably have been greatly embellished with the re-telling through the years. Some families are blessed (or cursed, depending on your viewpoint) with storytellers, some of whom may have been out-and-out fabricators. Or perhaps some of your forebears once upon a time spun yarns to entertain their children on cold snowy evenings in the long ago, pre-television, VCRs, video games and computer days. And, those children passed down the stories to their children and grandchildren as being true.

It is difficult to give up treasured family legends, but if you are going to be a good genealogist you must keep an open mind and be prepared to learn that some of the *facts* you have been told may be *fiction*.

No princesses

The Cherokees did not have royalty. So do not believe any *Cherokee Princess* legends. This is a term used by the English and colonial Americans, probably traceable in usage to stories pertaining to the famous daughter of a chief of the Powhatans known as Pocahontas. This inaccurate reference still appears in print in the works of historians, who ought to know better.

Among the legends you may encounter are those pertaining to the Trail of Tears and why your ancestors were or were not involved in this forced migration to Oklahoma. Most of us have a rather murky image of the entire removal story—formulated from movies, television, artists' conceptions of it and bits and pieces of American history. One of the best books on the history of this tribe is *The Cherokees* by Grace Steele Woodward. It was published by the University of Oklahoma Press and still is in print.

Trail of Tears

The removal actually started when about 17,000 Cherokees, who had refused to emigrate under the disputed Treaty of New Echota (1835), were rounded up at gun or bayonet point by soldiers and were placed into holding areas (pens), which were guarded. It is these stories of the harsh roundup that have become interwoven with the actual removal on the Trail of Tears. Early in June of 1838, the removal to what would later be Oklahoma started when approximately 2,800 of those who had been forcibly rounded up, were divided into three detachments, each accompanied by a military officer, a corps of assistants and two physicians. The first detachment of about 800—made up of

Cherokees from Georgia who had been concentrated at Ross's Landing (now Chattanooga)—departed 6 June. It was forcibly placed on boats and was under the command of Lt. Edward Deas. The second group, numbering about 875, left 13 June. It was under the command of Lt. R. H. K. Whiteley, with five assistant conductors, two physicians, three interpreters and a hospital attendant. The third contingent of 1,070 departed from Ross's Landing 17 June in wagons and on foot for Waterloo, Alabama, where they were to be transported on flatboats. After their departure, they learned that the removal of the remaining 13,000 Cherokees had been suspended until autumn because of the heat, drought and sickness. This third group asked to be allowed to return and remain with others in Tennessee, but their request was denied.

Chief vs. General

Major General Winfield Scott was in charge of the 7,000 federal and state troops whose job it was to round up and eject the Cherokees from their country in Georgia, Alabama, Tennessee and North Carolina. In the early part of July in 1838, when Chief John Ross returned to the Cherokee Nation from the nation's capital, where he had been negotiating unsuccessfully about the treaty and removal, he was able to persuade General Scott to permit the Cherokees to manage and control their own removal in the autumn. Thus, Ross gained a concession that was not granted to any other tribe that was removed, and as a result, the great majority of Cherokees who traveled the Trail of Tears were not guarded by soldiers.

The Cherokees were divided into 13 detachments averaging 1,000 each. Officers were appointed by the Cherokee council to take charge of the emigration, with two leaders in charge of each detachment and a sufficient number of wagons and horses for the purpose. To maintain order on the march each party established a quasi-police organization that punished infractions of regulations. They also had guides and provisioners to arrange for their food. They finally started west after the drought was broken in October of 1838. However, there was a party of Cherokees that belonged to the treaty faction (pro-removal) of the tribe who refused to emigrate under the leadership of Chief Ross. This group left the old nation on 11 October under the direction of Lt. Edward Deas.

Under the Treaty of New Echota, the Cherokees were assured that once they were settled in their new land in Indian Territory they would:

- Have their firearms restored to them once they were at or beyond the Mississippi River.
- Be paid for their improvements that they had left in the east.
- Be paid for their lost land.
- Be paid subsistence for six months to one year.

After the initial shock of the brutal roundup and imprisonment, most of them went with their families and friends to Indian Territory, and only four of the 17 contingents had U.S. Army escorts. It is estimated that about 4,000 Cherokees died from the time of the roundup until they reached what is now Oklahoma.

Other legends

There may be many other legends in your family. The only way to prove or disprove them is to use historical evidence and all the primary records you can find. Determine where your ancestors resided at particular time periods and then examine pertinent genealogical and historical records of that time and place. For example, if a family legend claims your Cherokee ancestor was from Ohio, a quick check of the map on page iv, which shows where Cherokee towns and settlements (1785–1838) were located, will tell you that Ohio was not home to this tribe. There are a number of excellent histories available (see bibliography) containing maps that show exactly where the Cherokee Nation's boundaries were and where the tribe resided at various dates.

Since most researchers are involved in the tracing of mixed-bloodlines, keep focused on determining when and where your Cherokee progenitors would have come in contact with your white ancestors. These white ancestors usually will turn out to be traders, missionaries, teachers or government agents. It is claimed that by 1830 almost one-quarter of all Cherokees had some white ancestors, with two out of three intermarriages involving a white man and a Cherokee woman. Intermarriage with blacks was rare, and after 1824, it was against Cherokee law.

Black Indians

Among the Cherokees who traveled the Trail of Tears were about 1,600 black slaves who were pushed westward along with their masters. Slave owners were mostly the mixed-bloods. After the Civil War most of these freed blacks remained in Indian Territory, and by and large remained in the nation in which they had lived as slaves. For many African American families with Native American ancestry, there often is a misconception that the first Indian ancestor to be found will be the one who is the full-blood.

Race was a significant factor with the Cherokees, and it can be most difficult to prove a mixed Cherokee-African American bloodline. In such cases, the Cherokee bloodline was frequently discounted at the time of the official enrollment. Genealogists should consult the Cherokee Freedmen records first. African Americans, even if they were part Cherokee, usually were classified as Cherokee Freedmen rather than Cherokee by Blood. An excellent book on this subject is by Angela Y. Walton-Riji entitled *Black Indian Genealogy Research.*

Short cut for some

If you find your Cherokee ancestors enumerated as Indians in the 1900 census, you can take a short cut. Extract all of the information from the enumerations and then go to the *Final Rolls of the Five Civilized Tribes.* These records and an index to them are on microfilm and are available at the National Archives, its Southwest Region Branch in Fort Worth, Texas, the Family History Library in Salt Lake City, American Genealogical

Lending Library in Ogden, Utah and at various academic libraries.

If you have access to *Dawes Roll "Plus" of Cherokee Nation, 1898* by Bob Blankenship, which was published in 1994, you can look for your Cherokee ancestors alphabetically by surname. This book is available in many libraries, and it includes the names of 36,714 Cherokee citizens by blood. Also there is a two-volume set entitled *The Final Rolls of Citizens and Freedmen of the Five Civilized Tribes in Indian Territory* and *Index to the Final Rolls of Citizens and Freedmen of the Five Civilized Tribes in Indian Territory,* available at various libraries, including the Family History Library in Salt Lake City.

The Final Roll is arranged numerically by enrollment; category is by tribe. It contains roll number, name, age, gender, quantum of blood, and census card number. *The Index to the Final Roll* is arranged alphabetically by surname under tribe categories; it will give you the name and roll number. Use the index first to find your ancestor. Then locate your ancestor in *The Final Roll,* and record the census card number. The census card is a family group as it existed when the final roll was made. If some of the older children in a family were already married they will have a census card of their own, so keep this in mind if you don't find all of the children listed. Also, there may have been children who were born after the final roll—between 1902 and 1906.

Census vs. roll numbers

Each census card has only one number—in the upper right-hand corner. Don't confuse this number with the roll number. You will discover that each family member had an individual roll number. Copies of the census cards can be obtained from:

1. National Archives-Southwest Region, P.O. Box 6216, Fort Worth, TX 76115.
2. Oklahoma Historical Society, Indian Archives, 2100 Lincoln Boulevard, Oklahoma City, OK 73105.

3. Family History Library, 35 North West Temple, Salt Lake City, UT 84150.

4. American Genealogical Lending Library, P.O. Box 244, Bountiful, UT 84011-0244.

Citizenship and bloodlines

The Dawes Roll continues to serve as the only basis for determining eligibility today for membership in the Cherokee Nation of Oklahoma. If your direct ancestors are not on this roll you are not are eligible. However, most genealogists are not so concerned with being a citizen of the tribe as simply proving their Cherokee heritage. It helps to know that Cherokee citizenship was not based exclusively on bloodlines as most genealogists assume. Your ancestor could have had Cherokee blood and still not have been a citizen of the Cherokee Nation. Some of our mixed-blood ancestors, in particular, left the tribe at different times for various reasons. The constitution of the Cherokee Nation stated that whenever any citizen removed with his effects out of the limits of the nation and became a citizen of any other government, then all of his rights and privileges as a citizen of the Cherokee Nation ceased. However, the national council of the tribe had power to re-admit persons to all the rights of citizenship, if they desired to return to the nation. However, they had to apply for such readmission—it was not automatic. If your ancestors left the nation and never returned or returned, but never bothered to re-apply for citizenship, your Cherokee connections can be difficult, often impossible, to prove.

Census cards

For researchers using the Family History Library (FHL) in Salt Lake City or its branches (Family History Centers), there are microfilm copies of the Dawes census cards, applications and index. If you do not have the roll number or access to the published index, you will find the index on FHL film number 962,366, item 1. Search it for the name of the person under the tribe and category (blood, intermarriage, freedman, new born, minor). The individual's roll number will be in the right-hand column. Then use FHL film number 908,371, item 2 to find this roll number in the left-hand column. The individual's name will be in the center column and the Dawes card number in the right-hand column. The application numbers are the same as the Dawes card numbers. Then to find the film number for the Dawes card and/or the application, check the Subject section of the Family History Library Catalog under Indians of North America—Oklahoma. Look for United States/Commission to the Five Civilized Tribes. You also can use *Native American Register: A Guide to Selected Federal and State Sources Available at the Family History Library,* compiled by G. Eileen Buchway, revised by Ken Nelson. It will be found in the reference section near the U.S./Canada Reference desk. The call number is US/CAN 970.1 B858n.

If you locate your ancestor in these records, then you should be able to find them (or their ancestors) on earlier Cherokee rolls. This will enable you to continue your search in additional records which are discussed later. However, for most researchers making the Cherokee connection will not be this easy.

A mini-history

To trace any of our forebears it is necessary to study their ethnic history. This is especially true for Cherokee ancestors. The records of genealogical value that have been generated pertaining to them can best be understood and located if you have an accurate knowledge of the history of Cherokees. You will find several references to such histories in the bibliography—read all you can find.

The Cherokees, linguistically related to the Iroquois, lived in the southeastern United States before their forced removal in 1838/9 to what was Indian Territory, now northeastern Oklahoma. They were the warlords of the southern Appalachian highlands who once bragged that "War is our beloved occupation."

By 1700 through trade, diplomacy and superiority in warfare they emerged as one of the most powerful tribes in the region. Each village was governed by a local council at which any resident, regardless of gender, was welcome to speak. Women not only participated in the council but decided the fate of war captives.

Matriarchal society

The Cherokees had a matriarchal society whereby descent was traced strictly through the mother's side of the family. A person belonged to his mother's clan and the most important and powerful man in a child's life, was not his father, but the mother's brothers. The maternal uncles had responsibility for discipline of the child and taught him about hunting and warfare. The women owned the dwellings and were in control of all the property.

Clan affiliation was inherited through the mother's line and marriage within a clan was strictly forbidden. The household was the basic unit of the Cherokee social organization and a newly married couple usually lived with the wife's family. The clan provided many important functions including care for orphans and the destitute, hospitality for visiting clan members from other towns and the avenging of wrongs committed against clan members.

Seven clans

There were seven clans. The number seven was sacred to the Cherokees, and it permeates legends, beliefs and customs of the tribe. Since no records were kept of clan membership, only a few Cherokees can identify their clan.

The clans were:

- ☐ **Blue** or **Panther** (sometimes known as **Wild Cat**). They made blue medicine from a special plant to keep the children well.

- ☐ **Long Hair** (also known as **The Twister, Hair Hanging Down** or **Wind**). They wore their hair in elaborate hairdos. The peace chief, who wore a white feather robe, was usually from this clan.

- ☐ **Bird** clan members were the messengers and keepers of the birds.

- ☐ **Paint** clan members were the sorcerers and medicine men and those who made red paint.

- ☐ **Deer** clan members were the fast runners, the hunters and keepers of the deer.

- ☐ **Wild Potato** (also known as **Blind Savannah, Bear** or **Raccoon**) were those who dug the wild potatoes to make flour for bread.

- ☐ **Wolf** was the largest and most prominent clan and provided most of the tribe's war chiefs. It was the only clan that could kill a wolf.

All crimes such as theft of religious objects, assault on a priest, arson, treason, witchcraft, homicide, incest, stealing from the dead and intermarrying within a clan were all punishable by death. The Cherokees believed that *blood revenge*—the practice to avenge the victim by taking the life of the murderer—had to be taken in order to free the soul of the victim and to let it pass from this world into the next.

Each village of the Cherokees had two governmental units— a white and a red government. In peacetime the white government was in control of all affairs of the village. In times of war all duties fell on the red government, which consisted of younger men who would do well in battle. The white government consisted of a chief of the tribe, his right-hand man, prime counselors (one from each clan), a council of elders, a chief speaker and the messengers. The red government consisted of the Great War Chief, his assistant, seven war counselors, a War Woman, the Chief War Speaker and messengers. The seven war counselors were in charge of declaring war, while the War Woman's position was to declare the fate of captives and prisoners that were taken. The messengers served as scouts.

Tall, athletic and handsome

The Cherokees were a tall, athletic and handsome people. Their good looks, posture and stamina were admired by the Europeans. Oval-headed and olive-colored, they did not have the high cheekbones and Roman noses of the Plains Indians. Both genders tattooed their faces, arms and bodies and wore silver arm bands, earrings and nose ornaments. The men shaved their faces and heads, except for a small topknot. For war and ceremonies the men also colored their faces with stripes and circles of red, black, ochre and blue earthen pigments.

In 1634 the Cherokees first met the British who had settled in Virginia, but it was not until the 1690s that they came in regular contact with the British settlements—in South Carolina. At that time every Cherokee town had a communal garden in which women, children and old men cultivated such things as corn, beans, melons, squash, sweet potatoes and Indian tobacco. The women worked together gathering fruits, nuts and berries and cultivating the vegetables. Food was shared from a town granary, where bushels were stored in cribs from harvest to harvest, plus each family had its own garden. The men cleared the fields for planting and helped out during harvesting, but they were often absent for three or four months at a time—fishing and hunting for deer, bear, turkey and rabbit.

White traders

Next to tobacco and timber, the most important sources of income for the British colonies were furs and hides, and the deer-skin trade once was a significant part of the Southern economy. As Cherokee men became more involved in trade, they gained the means to purchase hoes, metal kettles, cotton cloth or glass beads for their wives as European trade goods were greatly desired by the Cherokees. By 1714 white traders were making annual trading trips to the Cherokee towns, with some of them settling among the tribe and raising mixed-blood families. The traders naturally en-couraged the Cherokees to do more hunting for the animals that produced valuable furs and hides. By 1740 there were about 150 traders involved with the Cherokees.

The Cherokees did not have royalty or a national leader, so the English tried to create one as the whites preferred to deal with one in authority rather than making individual deals with various tribesmen. In 1721 the governor of South Carolina met with 37 Cherokee chiefs and persuaded them to make Chief Wrosetawastow their "king." And in later years a succession of chiefs were as-sumed, incorrectly by the English and later by Americans, to speak for the nation.

European diseases—smallpox, typhus, whooping cough and measles—caused more Cherokee deaths than all of the border raids and Indian wars. The failure of their medicine men to cure these diseases eroded faith in them and their rituals and probably ac-counts to some degree the Cherokees' early acceptance of the white man's ways. About half of the tribe died in a smallpox epidemic in 1738–39, decreasing its size to about 10,000.

Westward expansion

When the French and Indian War broke out in 1755, the Cherokees at first honored their alliance with England, but after several unprovoked assaults upon them by Carolina frontiersmen in 1760, some Cherokees switched sides. Large armies of frontiersmen invaded Cherokee towns, burning their houses and granaries and laying waste to crops and slaughtering men, women and children. The frontier settlers used the opportunity to drive the Cherokees west of the Appalachians, and in 1761 the Cherokees made peace on the English's terms.

England tried to halt the westward expansion of the American colonists by forbidding any settlements beyond the Appalachian Ridge. The British even surveyed the ridge line from Maine to Georgia and established superintendents among the Indians in an attempt to sustain the fur trade and keep the peace. Two assistant superintendents lived among the Cherokees. They were Alexander Cameron in the North Carolina mountains and John McDonald along the Tennessee River near what is now Chattanooga.

The Cherokees backed the British during the American Revolution, and as a result their chiefs were forced to sign treaties with the new and victorious American nation. They wound up ceding more than 8,000 square miles, and in 1785 in exchange for peace, the Cherokees made some crucial concessions—granting the United States sole and exclusive right of regulating the trade with them, managing all of their affairs, and acknowledged themselves "to be under the protection of the United States." The United States then sent a deputy of its choice to reside among the Cherokees as its agent. This first treaty with the new United States was concluded on the Keowee River at Hopewell, South Carolina on 28 November 1785.

Famous marks

The signatures and/or marks on this historical document are:

Benjamin Hawkins, And'w Pickens, Jos. Martin, Lach'n McIntosh, Koatohee (Corn Tassel) of Toquo, Scholauetta (Hanging Man) of Chota, Tuskegatahu (Long Fellow) of Chistohoe, Ooskwha (Abraham) of Chilkowa, Kolakusta (Prince of Noth), Newota (Gritzs) of Chicamaga, Konatota (Rising Fawn) of Highwassay, Tuckasee (Young Terrapin) of Allajoy,

Toostaka (the Waker) of Oostanawa, Untoola (Gun Rod) of
Seteco, Unsuokanail (Buffalo White Calf), New Cussee,
Kostayeak (Sharp Fellow Wa-taga), Chonosta of Cowe,
Chescoonwho (Bird in Close) of Tomotlug, Tuckasee (Terrapin)
of Hightowa, Chesetoa (the Rabbit) of Tlacoa, CheSecotetona
(Yellow Bird) of the Pine Log, Sketaloska (Second Man) of
Tillico, Chokasatahe (Chickasaw Killer Ta-sonta), Onanoota of
Koosoate, Ookoseta (Sower Mush) of Koo-loque, Umatooeth
(Water Hunter), Choikamawga, Wyuka of Lookout Mountain,
Tulco (Tom) of Chatuga, Will of Akoha, Necatee of Sawta,
Amokontakona (Kutcloa), Kowetatahee, of Frog Town,
Keukuck (Talcoa), Tulatiska of Chaway, Wooaluka (Waylayer),
Chota, Tatliusta (Porpoise) of Tilassi, John of Little Tallico,
Skelelak, Akonoluchta (the Cabin), Cheanoka of Kawetakac, and
Yellow Bird. Witnesses were: Wm. Blount, Sam'l Taylor, major;
John Owen, Jess. Walton, Jno. Cowan, Capt. Comm'd't;
Thos. Gregg, W. Hazzard, James Madison, Arthur Cooley, sworn
interpreters.

After the Revolutionary War, the Cherokee leaders realized
that they could no longer exist if they continued to pursue their
old way of life. The new American president, George Washington,
promised them hoes, plows, horses and cattle, and with increased
competition from white hunters and a diminishing supply of deer
and beaver, Cherokee men began to give up hunting and the fur
trade in favor of herding livestock and raising cash crops for
market.

Role of mixed-bloods

From about the 1730s until the outbreak of the American
Revolution the Cherokees had intermarried with Scots, English,
Germans and Irish—mostly traders among them. From these
mixed-blood unions of the Colonial period would later come many
of the Cherokee leaders. Not all mixed-blood consortia were
legalized by even the pretense of a Cherokee wedding ceremony,
but many were. The offspring of these mixed-blood marriages or
consortia played a major role in influencing the Cherokees to
become "civilized" and do things the way the whites did. By 1796

among the Cherokees were the Doughertys, Galpins and Adairs (Irish); Rosses, Vanns and McIntoshes (Scottish).

The Cherokees began to make progress in agriculture, animal husbandry and mechanical skills as well as in education and government. Agents were appointed by both Presidents Washington and Adams, as provided by the Treaty of Holston, and they resided among the Cherokees and engaged carpenters, wheelwrights, smiths and weavers to teach the Cherokees various crafts. The white man's religion was rejected until about 1800 when the Moravians established a school within the nation. In 1803 the chiefs and headmen agreed to let the Rev. Gideon Blackburn, a young minister from Tennessee, establish a mission school in the Overhills country near Tellico, Tennessee.

Land cessions

Between 1791 and 1819 the Cherokees negotiated 25 land cessions with the federal government. The major reason for these land cessions was debt. The Cherokees fell into debt to the United States—having purchased more goods and supplies from both private trading companies and a Cherokee factory at Tellico, Tennessee, than they could pay for. Factory goods were often forced on the Cherokees by the factor (storekeeper) and many of their chiefs were corrupted through bribery. President John Adams was first to arrange for the revocation of the Cherokee debts in exchange for cessions of land. Between 1819 and 1827 the Cherokee Nation adopted as its main objective the preservation and protection of its remaining lands. In 1821 the Cherokee syllabary, invented about four years earlier, by one of the tribe's most renowned citizens—Sequoyah—was accepted by the tribe, and almost over night the tribe became literate.

Compact of 1802

In an effort to forestall the removal of their people from ancestral homelands that had been promised to the state of Georgia by the Compact of 1802, progressive Cherokee leaders, many of whom were mixed-bloods, undertook an ambitious and aggressive program. It was one designed to further Cherokee education and religion and replace ancient Cherokee culture with that of the white man's, and one that would convert the Cherokee's tribal government into a republic, patterned after that of the United States. By doing so the Cherokees hoped to convince the United States that the nation merited respect; and that it would then, they hoped, bring its 1802 compact with Georgia to a close by a compromise or another method other than that of extinguishing the Cherokees' title to their lands in that area. In 1802 Thomas Jefferson's administration made a pact with Georgia whereby that state was to cede her western land to the United States and receive $1,250,000 in payment for the same, along with the guarantee that the United States would extinguish, at its own expense, for the use of Georgia as early as the same could be peaceably obtained upon reasonable terms, the Indian title to the lands lying within the limits of that state. This Georgia Compact of 1802 was **the** threat to the Cherokee Nation's land for more than 30 years, and eventually was responsible for the forced removal of the tribe to what is now Oklahoma.

The Bowl and Duwali

A group of Cherokees who had fought on the British side during the American Revolution, petitioned the Spanish governor at New Orleans in 1782 for permission to settle on the west side of the Mississippi within Spanish territory, and this permission was granted. In 1794 a group of Cherokees under *The Bowl*, their leader, settled in the Saint Francis River Valley, located in what is now southeastern Missouri. Other Cherokees joined them from time to time. In December of 1811 a great earthquake occurred in this area. It was so intense that it caused the Mississippi River to flow backwards for more than a mile and submerged much of the area. Aftershocks occurred for some time frightening the inhabitants. During the winter of 1811–12, the Cherokees living in this area moved en masse to territory between the Arkansas and White rivers in present-day Arkansas. Eventually other Cherokees who decided to emigrate from the old nation in the east joined them in what was called the Arkansas country.

Additionally, the region of Texas adjacent to Arkansas and Louisiana became a popular place for southeastern Indians, including Cherokees, as well as for American frontiersmen. In the winter of 1819–1820, the first Cherokees known to have settled permanently in Texas crossed the Red River. Their leader was probably *Duwali*, a Western Cherokee chief. The next year he and his followers relocated their village further westward at the Three Forks of the Trinity River, then later moved into the uninhabited region north of Nacogdoches, where others of the Western Cherokees under *Blanket, Takatoka* and *Tahchee* joined them.

After Texas won its independence from Mexico, the Cherokees learned they were not welcome in Texas. Therefore, for most of them the stay in Texas was brief and they rejoined their fellow tribesmen, known as the Western Cherokees or Old Settlers in Indian Territory.

Treaty of New Echota

While some Cherokees had voluntarily removed west of the Mississippi River prior to 1835, most of the tribe remained on their ancestral lands in Georgia, Tennessee, Alabama and North Carolina. They were well informed on political matters as the Cherokee Nation began publishing an official national newspaper—the *Cherokee Phoenix*—in 1828. In the 1830s the Cherokees were divided about removal. Some were determined to resist at all costs, while others believed that the best they could hope for was to negotiate a fair price for their land and compensation for transportation costs to the West. The leaders of the latter group met with President Andrew Jackson's representatives in 1835 and signed the Treaty of New Echota, in which they relinquished claim to their ancestral lands. About 15,000 Cherokees, including many women and children, petitioned the United States to reject the treaty, but their pleas went unheeded. When the time came to carry out the eviction in 1838 most Cherokees refused to move. At the time of the disputed Treaty of New Echota in 1835 the Cherokees who lived east of the Mississippi resided in what are now all or parts of the following counties of Georgia, Alabama, Tennessee and North Carolina:

- **Georgia**—Cass, Catoosa, Chattanooga, Cherokee, Cobb, Dade, Dawson, Fannin, Floyd, Forsyth, Gilmer, Gordon, Haralson, Lumpkin, Murray, Paulding, Pickens, Polk, Towns, Union, Walker and Whitfield.

- **Alabama**—Blount, Cherokee, Dekalb, Etowah, Jackson and Marshall.

- **Tennessee**—Bradley, Hamilton, Polk, Marion, Meigs, Monroe and Polk.

- **North Carolina**—Cherokee, Clay, Graham, Macon and Swain.

If your families were not in these areas in the 1830s or in what is now Arkansas, Oklahoma or Texas, the likelihood of finding or proving a Cherokee connection is greatly diminished. If your families were in Georgia, Alabama, Tennessee or North Carolina, you will want to consult the *Register of Persons Who Wish Reservations Under the Treaty of 1817,* which has been published and is also on microfilm at the Family History Library. This register consists of those persons who took a life reservation (640 acres) under the treaties of 1817 and 1819. Copies of these claim papers—often rich in genealogical data—can be obtained from the National Archives. On the 1835 census of the Cherokees if an individual was a reservee, it would be so noted, and if the reservee was deceased in 1835, his or her heirs were designated as descendants of reservees.

Among the remarks found in this record are such things as *Spaniard, native, in right of her children, in right of his wife, enrolled for Arkansas,* as well as place of residence being noted. Judging from the number of non-Cherokee surnames in this record, it appears that many of the mixed-bloods took reservations. You also will want to consult *Cherokee Reservees,* compiled by David Keith Hampton. In it he notes the 156 heads of Cherokee families who enlisted for reservations under the conditions stated in the Treaty of 1817. The provision that they would receive a life reservation meant they were not able to sell their land or hold on to it if they moved elsewhere, but their children would accrue those rights after the parent died. Since many of these individuals were intermarried whites, this provision gave some protection to their Cherokee children.

Cherokee reservees

A new treaty in 1819 granted reservations to 155 additional families. The Treaty of 1819 also made provisions for Cherokee families who it was felt could handle their own affairs and under this provision 39 persons received reservations in fee simple. These people were specifically named in the treaty, and nine of them were given reservations on which they did not reside.

But from the beginning the Cherokee families who lived on the ceded lands had trouble with their white neighbors and various state governments. There are some horror stories related in the files of the reservees who were often run off their own properties. In Tennessee an act was passed providing for the survey of all the Cherokee lands in the state and these lands were eventually sold with no provision made for the life estates received by the Cherokees. In 1820 and 1821 those Indians who had remained in Tennessee were evicted from their lands. The state of Georgia passed laws to bring all of the Indian lands in its borders into its control, even those not yet ceded by treaty. North Carolina did not act directly against the holders of life reservations, but neither did it make any provisions for them when the land was surveyed and releases were eventually obtained from the reservees for inadequate consideration in most instances. The state of Alabama never asserted any rights against the reservees, but most of this land eventually fell into the hands of white individuals. In some instances it was by purchase, with neither party realizing the Cherokee reservee did not have the right to sell the land. The United States was finally forced to purchase the reservations from some of those who were illegally evicted from their lands in Georgia, North Carolina and Alabama.

Four commissions were eventually formed to hear Cherokee grievances not only related to the reservations but to various other aspects of the Cherokees' forced removal of 1838/9. While some

Cherokee claimants were able to prove they had followed the provisions of the treaties and were compensated for their losses, most were not and wound up with nothing. Claim papers relating to decisions of the four commission boards are in the National Archives in Washington, D.C., and copies may be obtained from it. They are in the records of the Bureau of Indian Affairs (Record Group 75).

Intra-tribal problems

The Cherokees had their intra-tribal political problems after the removal. In June of 1839 three chiefs of the Eastern Cherokees—John Ross, George Lowrey and Edward Gunter—met with leaders of the Western Cherokees—John Brown, John Looney and John Rogers—to draft new laws and to unite the two governments. In a treaty with the United States in 1828, the Western Cherokees ceded their lands in Arkansas for lands in what is now Oklahoma. They did not have a written constitution and only a few written laws. Their capital was at Tahlonteskee, located on the Illinois River. The Western Cherokees divided their nation into four districts and the Cherokee Nation West consisted of seven million acres adjacent to Missouri on the northeast and to Arkansas on the east, with a neutral strip fifty miles wide and twenty-five miles deep dividing Missouri from the Osage Nation to the west. In addition to farming and hunting the Western Cherokees owned and operated grist mills and saltworks. The Western Cherokees are also known as the Old Settler Cherokees.

On 6 September 1839 a new constitution was formally adopted by the Cherokee council, which then was comprised of both Eastern and Western Cherokees at an assembly held at Tahlequah, their new capital. At this council John Ross was unanimously elected principal chief of the Cherokee Nation and David Vann, a Western Cherokee, was elected assistant or second chief. Thus the Cherokees were reunited with the exception of the small group that escaped during the roundup-removal and hid in the mountains. The descendants of the latter group still live in North Carolina.

The Cherokees were greatly divided during the Civil War and lost more land to the U.S. government because of the support many of its tribe gave to the Confederacy.

Districts of the Cherokee Nation

The Cherokee Nation was divided into districts—Delaware, Saline, Tahlequah, Goingsnake, Flint, Illinois, Cooweescoowee, Canadian and Skin Bayou. The latter eventually became Sequoyah District. Each of these districts had a courthouse where the district's business was conducted. Each district had a judge, two senators, three councilors, and a clerk, solicitor and sheriff. Records of the districts (similar to modern-day counties) were kept in the courthouses, and they included marriage, divorce, probate and guardianship records, as well as various criminal proceedings. Among the districts' files are records pertaining to whites also, such as work permits and those who were considered to be intruders (squatters) who did not have permission to reside in the nation. Some of these records date as early as 1848 and as late as 1904.

After Oklahoma became a state in 1907 these former Cherokee districts became the following counties in northeastern Oklahoma: Washington, Nowata, Craig, Rogers, Delaware, Mayes, Cherokee, Adair, Sequoyah and part of Muskogee County.

Prior to 1896 the Cherokee Nation had jurisdiction over its own citizenship and over non-Indians who were living in its tribal territory—those who were allowed to live and work therein.

Permit records

Intruders and permit records of the Cherokee districts have been microfilmed and are available at the Indian Archives, Oklahoma Historical Society, Archives and Manuscripts in Oklahoma City. They also can be accessed at the National Archives, the Fort Worth, Texas, regional branch of the National Archives, as well as through several other repositories. The permit records can help you locate white ancestors who were in the

Cherokee Nation prior to Oklahoma's statehood. This is important because if your white ancestors were residing in the Cherokee
Nation between 1840–1900 that may explain why you have been
unable to find them on federal censuses for a particular date.

Sources and records

The 1860 slave schedule for Arkansas (M653, roll 54) and
what is labeled "Indian lands west of Arkansas" contains names
of the Cherokee slave owners. Often you will find "Ind." (for Indian) after their names. There also is a population schedule for
this same area (M653, roll 52), which includes only whites and
free blacks, so a comparison between the two enumerations can
help distinguish the slave owners with American surnames who
were Indians.

The permit records indicate the name of the person under
permit, the number in his family, type of work he was hired for,
period of time for work and who the Cherokee citizen was that
took out the permit, along with the cost of the permit. Intruders—
those who were in the Cherokee Nation without a permit—can be
found on lists dated as early as 1859. An intruder was given a
certain time to vacate his improvements and time to leave. The
improvements were then put up for sale to the highest Cherokee
citizen bidder.

The Cherokee Nation was a self-governing one until 1906,
just prior to Oklahoma statehood. The tribe had its own agent
from the Office of Indian Affairs (OIA) until the Union Agency
was set up in Muskogee (now Oklahoma) about 1874. In the early
1900s this agency became an area office of the OIA, later called
the Bureau of Indian Affairs (BIA).

Dawes Commission

In 1893 President Grover Cleveland appointed a commis-
sion to meet with the Five Civilized Tribes—Cherokee, Creek,
Choctaw, Chickasaw and Seminole. The purpose was to get the
Indians to relinquish their surplus lands west of the 96th meridian

and to make room for settlement of non-Indians under the Homestead laws. Henry L. Dawes, former U.S. senator from Massachusetts, was named to head this commission. The commission was to obtain an agreement with the tribes to take allotments of land in severalty. (An estate in severalty is one that is held by a person in his own right only, without any other person being joined or connected with him.) Until this time, Cherokee lands had always been held by the tribe, not by individuals of the tribe. The commission was also asked by the federal government to make an agreement with the Five Civilized Tribes to give up their tribal governments. At that time each of these tribes had its own constitution and government as a separate nation.

In 1896 the Dawes Commission was authorized to receive applications for enrollment in addition to persons already on tribal rolls. It was at this time that the decision of citizenship claims was taken out of the control of the Indian courts and given to this commission. As a result many records were created which are of great interest to genealogists. When word got out that the lands of the Five Civilized Tribes were to be divided and allotted, thousands of claimants came forward who claimed to be of Indian descent and demanded a right to share in the distribution of tribal lands and monies. Each of these claims had to be investigated. Many claims were without foundation, yet the commission had to give serious consideration to each until it was proven to be either true or false. The commission enrolled all the Indians in each of the tribes, as well as all of the freedmen of each tribe. The freedmen were the African Americans, who as slaves had belonged to the Indians before the abolition of slavery. The surviving freedmen, as well as all descendants of freedmen, were entitled to the allotment of lands according to the U.S. government.

Allotting 20 million acres

The allotment of Indian lands was a difficult and tedious procedure. First the lands had to be classified and the valuation placed upon each tract in order that individual allotments might be properly apportioned and equalized as to value. An allotee could choose a homestead at one place, then could also choose one or more additional tracts of land to complete the total value apportioned. Some Native Americans refused to choose an allotment, in which case, the commission selected the land to be allotted.

The Dawes Commission had its headquarters and main office at Muskogee, Oklahoma (then located in the Creek Nation, Indian Territory). Due to the scope of its work, some of the workers had to go into the field and set up camp. Even before the creation of the Dawes Commission, surveyors had begun their work surveying the land of what was then Oklahoma and Indian Territories.

This commission's two main duties were:

1. To determine who were the bona fide citizens or heirs entitled to inherit the some 20 million acres that had been surveyed and set aside for allotment.
2. To take an inventory of the properties to be divided.

To determine tribal citizens or heirs, the commission heard from more than 200,000 claimants. All of these cases had to be made matters of record, many of them involving hundreds of pages of evidence and pleadings. Eventually 101,211 were certified to share in the properties of the Five Civilized Tribes. They were enrolled up to and including 4 March 1907.

Of the number certified, the final breakdown of Cherokees were:

FULL BLOODS: 6,601
PART BLOODS: 29,975*
*(includes 197 registered Delawares)
INTERMARRIED: 286
FREEDMEN: 4,923
TOTAL: 41,785

By the close of the 1907 allotments had been made to the majority of the citizens and freedmen of the Five Civilized Tribes. Work that year consisted mainly of making allotments to minor children enrolled under the Act of Congress approved 26 April 1906, and to those citizens and freedmen previously enrolled but who had not selected the entire amount of land to which they were entitled. More than 4,400,000 acres were allotted to Cherokees and connected Delawares in accordance with the agreement ratified by an act of Congress of 1 July 1902 and approved by the tribe on 7 August 1902.

Under that agreement, each member of the tribe received land equal in value to 110 acres of average allottable land, which included a homestead equal to 40 acres of average allottable land. Freedmen received 40 acres of land. Many applications for enrollment through intermarriage were permitted to make tentative allotment selections pending a final decision on enrollment. When the U. S. Supreme Court ruled against the intermarried Cherokees on 5 November 1906, most relinquished their selections to their minor children who were enrolled.

Many Cherokee full-bloods, called Night Hawks, refused to make selections and were allotted land arbitrarily by the commission. The first deeds to Cherokee allotments were delivered in June of 1906 and equalization payments began in 1910. Once the applications for citizenship were reviewed by the Dawes Commission, the final rolls were prepared.

Dawes Commission records

These enrollment applications contain much genealogical information. They are microfilmed and can be found at National Archives, its Southwest Regional branch at Fort Worth, Texas, the Family History Library of Salt Lake City and through American Genealogical Lending Library (AGLL). Call or microfilm numbers given are those designated either by National Archives or Family History Library. The latter are referenced as FHL film and a number. AGLL uses National Archives' references.

☐ Enrollment cards of the Dawes Commission (also known as census cards) are available on microfilm (M1186) for the Five Civilized Tribes, 1898–1914. Roll 1 is the index to the final roll. FHL film numbers for those pertaining to Cherokees are numbers 1,022,530 (item 3 through 1,023,034, item 1). Categories include: Cherokee by blood, by marriage, and minors; freedmen and freedmen minors. They include Delawares adopted by the Cherokees, as well as rejected and doubtful applications. Information includes: name, age, sex, relationship to the head of household, enrollment number, if approved, parents' names, degree of Indian blood.

☐ There also is an index (7RA24) to Cherokee rejected and doubtful Dawes enrollment cards (often of great value to genealogists). The archives at Fort Worth is unable to undertake the research required to determine if a specific individual was enrolled. However, it can provide copies of enrollment cards and documents from the related applications jacket if you provide the enrollee's name, tribe, enrollment number and card number. The charge was about $6 per card number (for up to 24 pages) and your check or money order should be made payable to the National Archives Trust Fund.

Researchers using the Family History Library in Salt Lake City should consult either *Native American Register*, to be found in the reference area near the U.S./Canada desk or do the following:

☐ Search the index on FHL film No. 962,366, item 1, for the name of the person under the tribe and category. Categories are: blood, intermarriage, freedmen, newborn, and minors. The individual's roll number is in the right-hand column.

☐ Look at FHL film No. 908,371, item 2 and find the person's roll number in the left-hand column. On this film, the individual's name is in the center column and the Dawes card number is in the right-hand column.

Application numbers are the same as the Dawes card numbers. To find the film number for the Dawes card and/or the application, look in the **subject section** of the Family History Library Catalog under United States/Indians of North America/Oklahoma/Commission to the Five Civilized Tribes. You also can find the appropriate film number by consulting *Native American Register.*

Final rolls—final authority

The Dawes Final Rolls continues to serve as the only basis for determining eligibility for membership today in the Cherokee Nation of Oklahoma and for receiving benefits through that tribe. There were originally more than 30,000 entries. However, many were stricken from the roll because of death, non-citizenship or as duplicate entries. An act of Congress of 1 August 1914 added 127 more names to this section. Because all members of one household generally shared a census card number, an educated guess about family relationships may be made by observing the ages and blood degrees.

Minor Cherokees by Blood refers to those children born between 1902 and 1906 whose parents were either enrolled or had applications pending. The records list the individual's name, age in 1906, sex, blood degree, and census card number for 4,991 children.

Intermarried Cherokees, Cherokee Freedmen and Minor Cherokee Freedmen categories provide the individual's name, roll number, age, sex and census card number. Although many people appear as intermarried whites on the census cards, only 286 persons are on the roll as Intermarried Cherokees because citizenship was granted to only those married prior to 1877.

A payment was made in 1962 to living Cherokee individuals whose ancestor appeared on the Dawes Roll. It was necessary at that time to complete a *Proof of Death and Heirship* application. If you know of any relative (aunt, uncle, parent or cousin) who received this payment, they can identify the ancestor on the Dawes Roll.

The Delaware Cherokees

Delaware Cherokees references 197 persons who were adopted into the Cherokee tribe. Information includes the individual's name, roll number, age, sex, blood degree and census card number.

Guion Miller Rolls

In 1905, the Eastern Cherokees were awarded a $1 million settlement for their claims against the United States. A special agent of the Interior Department, Guion Miller, was given the task to compile a roll of eligible persons.

Guion Miller Rolls are an excellent source, even if your ancestors did not receive any of the funds. Many mixed-bloods genealogies can be found in these applications made to the U.S. Court of Claims to participate in the distribution of funds due to the Eastern Cherokees under the treaties of 1835–36 and 1845. This distribution of funds was made to all Cherokees who were alive on 28 May 1906, except those who had moved west prior to 1835, and who could establish the fact that at the time of the treaties they or their ancestors were members of the Eastern Cherokee tribe and had not been affiliated with any other tribe.

Guion Miller submitted his report and the roll on 5 January 1910. His roll gives the application number, the Dawes Commission number from the *Final Rolls*, names by family group, address, relationship to the head of the family and their ages in 1906.

In order to qualify, persons had to meet these requirements:

☐ Were alive on 28 May 1906.

☐ Were members of the Eastern Cherokee Tribe at the time of the Treaty of New Echota in 1835, or were descendants of such persons.

☐ Had not been affiliated with any tribe of Indians other than the Eastern Cherokees or the Cherokee Nation (Western).

The Guion Miller Rolls (Eastern Cherokee Applications of the U.S. Court of Claims, 1906–1910) are on microfilm (M1104, 348 rolls). They also have been abstracted by Jerry Wright Jordan in an eight-volume series entitled *Cherokee By Blood,* and published by Heritage Books of Bowie, Maryland.

Cherokee Nation of Oklahoma

To determine whether you are eligible to be a member of the Cherokee Nation of Oklahoma (not the Eastern Band of Cherokees in North Carolina) you must:

☐ Locate your **direct** ancestor (aunts, uncles and cousins do not count) on the Dawes Roll.

☐ Once you have found your direct ancestor, then it is your responsibility to prove your relationship to that enrollee.

☐ Submit an application for a CDIB (Certificate of Degree of Indian Blood) card and Cherokee National of Oklahoma membership at the same time. The tribal registration office is the judge as to what proof is necessary to document your claim. The CDIB card is important to those wishing to claim Indian preference for government contracts or for receiving certain benefits.

☐ Certified birth certificates offer the most acceptable proof of birth and parentage, but are not acceptable proof of blood degree—**the Dawes Roll is the only authority accepted for that information.** In cases of adoption, the registration office considers only the biological parents.

☐ Complete the application for CDIB and tribal membership; list the correct roll number(s) from the

Dawes Roll for the ancestor you are tracing back to; attach a copy of your state-certified birth certificate or a copy of your Delayed Certificate of Birth (it must be signed and sealed by the state registrar). Probate records can be used in lieu of a state-certified birth certificate. These generally would involve the probate of the enrollee's land and the legal determination of his or her heirs. Submit state-certified copies of birth or death certificates for your non-enrolled ancestors that you are tracing through.

Send the completed applications and documents to:

Cherokee National Registration Office
P.O. Box 948
Tahlequah, OK 74465.

Note: If an applicant is not enrolled, a certified copy of birth certificate is required to establish relationship to an enrolled parent. If parents are not enrolled, a certified copy of birth certificate on each parent is also required. In some cases where the grandparents are not enrolled, a certified copy of birth certificate of each such grandparent will be required. Hospital or county-issued birth certificates are not acceptable. Death certificates may be used with a supporting affidavit. Copies of court proceedings probating the estate of your deceased ancestors are preferable in lieu of a birth certificate. If there have been such proceedings, submit a copy of same with the application.

Quick checklist

- List those ancestors you believe were Cherokees and who were alive between 1893 and 1907.
- Were they living in Indian Territory (eastern Oklahoma) in the 1900 and/or 1910 censuses?
- **Yes?** Check the index to the Dawes Roll.
- **No?** Check the index to the Guion Miller Roll.

If found on Dawes Roll:

- Note the person's enrollment number and category (by blood, minor, etc.).
- Find the person's card number.
- Find the enrollment card on M1186 (93 rolls).
- Use the information from the card to search the 1880 or 1896 Cherokee censuses. Then check earlier Cherokee rolls for your ancestors. See *American Indians: A Select Catalog of National Archives Microfilm Publications* and the rolls and census records of Cherokees to be found under that topic later in this book.

If not on Dawes Roll:

- Check the index to the Rejected Applicants. If you find them there, then find the person's card number, enrollment card on M1186 and use the information from the card to search the 1880 and 1896 Cherokee censuses and earlier rolls.
- If you do not find them on the Rejected Applicants, then check the Intruder Lists. If you find them there, they were not recognized by the Cherokees as a member of the tribe.

Jf found on Guion Miller Roll:

- You can obtain a copy of the person's application by send-
  ing the application number to: National Archives, Seventh and Pennsylvania Avenue, NW., Washington, DC
  20408.

Jf not found on Guion Miller Roll:

- Your ancestor may have Cherokee blood, but you may
  never be able to prove it because they evidently were
  never listed on any tribal roll or roll made by the federal
  government.

Unenrolled ancestors

Not every person with Cherokee heritage will be found on
the official rolls. However, failure to locate your ancestor on one
does not mean they did not have Cherokee blood or that you should
give up searching for them. It just means your search will be more
difficult. And, you should be prepared to spend a lifetime—if it is
important to you—in this pursuit.

The *Final Rolls of the Five Civilized Tribes* are final in every
respect. Whatever the *Dawes Roll* says, no matter how obvious
the error, is fact. Therefore, unless a person or their direct ancestor
appears on the *Dawes Roll* he/she cannot be considered legally to
be a member of any of the Five Civilized Tribes. Yet, on these
rolls are cases where full siblings are shown as having different
blood degrees. This probably resulted because of various government policies or plain old human errors. Remember these rolls
were compiled before computers and scanners were invented.

There is a possibility that your ancestor is on some other
section of the *Dawes Roll*. While the commission did not know-
ingly allow persons of mixed Indian blood to enroll with more
than one tribe, there are some dual enrollees. For example, a person of mixed Cherokee and Creek blood should only be on the
rolls of one tribe. However, mistakes were made.

Residential requirements

Other possibilities exist which might have prevented your Cherokee ancestors from appearing on the Dawes Roll. One was that it was a requirement for the enrollee to physically reside in Indian Territory (northeastern Oklahoma) at the time of enrollment. This rule excluded many Cherokees residing in other states. Additionally, the applicant had to submit proof of citizenship by citing a previous enrollment (generally the 1880 or 1896 rolls), which in turn meant the applicant, or their ancestor, had to have lived in Indian Territory at an earlier time. Also, some Cherokees, mostly the conservative Night Hawks—*Keetoowahs*—simply refused to participate in the enrollment and allotment procedures, and while they were eventually forced to enroll, it is likely that some never did, while others gave erroneous information.

And, it is quite possible that your ancestor applied to the Dawes Commission and was denied. More than 250,000 people sought enrollment in one of the Five Civilized Tribes, but the commission only approved slightly more than 101,000 applications. Be sure to examine the *Denied* and *Rejected* census cards

Before you give up

There are many miscellaneous records that may enable you to find your Cherokee ancestors—even though they may not be on the Dawes Roll. Here are some possibilities:

- There are some Cherokee Muster Rolls of 1838. These name the head of family and total number in the family or numbers of males and females over or under 21. These rolls have been published in Maud Bliss Allen's *Census Records and Cherokee Muster Rolls,* and also this is available on FHL film No. 908,999, item 2.

- The Moravian Church had missions among the Cherokees as early as 1737. The original records

(written in both German and English) are at the
Moravian Archives in Bethlehem, Pennsylvania. The following pertaining to the Cherokee Missions are on two
rolls of microfilm at the Family History Library.

Dates FHL film No.

1737–1766; 1783–1837	1,017,704
1801–1832 (Springplace, Georgia)	1,017,705
1823–1831 (Oochgelogy, Georgia)	1,017,705
1805–1862	1,017,705

- A list of more than 450 persons who obtained marriage
  licenses issued by the Cherokee Nation was published in
  the *Chronicles of Oklahoma* 6:19–28 in "Intermarried-
  Whites in the Cherokee National Between the Years 1865
  and 1887" by A. H. Murchison.

- Names of ferries and owners are mentioned in "Early
  Cherokee Ferry Crossings of the Eastern Tennessee River
  Basin," by Tony Holmes in *The Journal of East Tennes-
  see History,* Volume 62 (1990).

- Indian Pioneer Papers, 1860–1935. This University of
  Oklahoma Western history collection is on 1,012 micro-
  fiche and contains interviews of people married to Native
  Americans living on or near a reservation, and has valuable information concerning life in Oklahoma Territory.
  There is a general index. FHL fiche numbers 6016865-
  6016981.

Local and tribal histories

You can not read too many books about the history of this
tribe (and they are numerous) or the local histories of the counties
and states where it has resided. Historians often mention the
names of white traders, missionaries, teachers and government
agents, along with the names of the Cherokees. For example, in
Cherokee Renascence in the New Republic by William G.
McLoughlin the author mentions the Cherokee chiefs involved in
an 1819 conspiracy who lived in northeastern Alabama. They

were George Fields, Turtle Fields, The Speaker, Wasosey, Bear Meat, John Brown, The Mink, Parched Corn Flour, George Guess (Sequoyah), Young Wolf, Arch Campbell, Night Killer, James Spencer, and Captain John Thompson, who was also interpreter and scribe for the group. Historians' footnotes and bibliographies are a rich source of material that you may wish to obtain through your local public and academic libraries.

Military records

The National Archives has records containing information about Native Americans who served as soldiers. You may find references to your Cherokee ancestors in these. These include:

- ☐ Registers of enlistments in the U.S. Army, 1798–1914 (M233), Roll 70 is Indian Scouts, 1866–1877. Roll 71, Indian Scouts, 1878–1914.

- ☐ Compiled service records of military units in volunteer Civil War Union organizations, M594; Rolls 77–91 includes Indian Home Guards.

- ☐ National Archives M258, Rolls 77–91 are compiled service records of Confederate soldiers, units of Cherokee, Choctaw, Chickasaw, Creek, Osage and Seminole.

- ☐ Compiled records show service of military units in Confederate organizations M861; Roll 74 contains information on Indian units.

Tribal designations

Eastern Cherokees—This reference is to the main group of Cherokees who lived in Tennessee, Georgia, Alabama and North Carolina prior to the forced removal in 1838. This is not the same as the Eastern Band of Cherokees of North Carolina.

Western Cherokees (also called **Old Settlers** or **Emigrant Cherokees**)—These references are to those of the tribe who went west, first to Missouri and Arkansas and then Oklahoma prior to

Cherokee Connections

the Trail of Tears in 1838/9. The earliest official record of most of them is the 1851 Drennen Roll.

Eastern Band of Cherokees—This group has its origins in 1819 when a few families left the main body of the tribe and settled outside the nation. At the time of the forced removal, the Eastern Band claimed citizenship with the State of North Carolina and sought exemption under a clause in the Treaty of New Echota that allowed any Cherokee to remain in the East, if they were "qualified" and "desirous to become citizens of the states where they reside." Some fugitives from the forced removal joined this group, nearly tripling its size.

By 1868 their status as North Carolina citizens was still not completely resolved. The Eastern Band incorporated under North Carolina state law in 1889, but their status was not resolved until later. It fact, it was not until 1920 that they gained undisputed right to vote. In 1908 a controversial roll by Frank C. Churchill was compiled of the Eastern Band of Cherokees. In 1924, when the final disposition of the affairs of this group was done, the Baker Roll was compiled and became the basis for membership in the group. Original enrollees and their descendants born on or before 21 August 1957, possessing 1/32 degree Eastern Cherokee blood qualified—provided they applied before 14 August 1963, and either they or their parents maintained and dwelt in a home on the Qualla Reservation sometime between 4 June 1924 and 21 August 1957, and were not enrolled as members of another tribe. Persons born after 21 August 1957, or applying after 14 August 1963, were required to have 1/16 degree Eastern Cherokee blood. Membership application forms may be obtained from the Eastern Band of Cherokee Office Headquarters, Cherokee Enrollment Office, P.O. Box 455, Cherokee, NC 28719.

Genealogists interested in these families should consult *Cherokee Roots* by Bob Blankenship. It includes a name index to the various rolls taken of the Eastern Band and can save you time and effort. The Eastern Band of Cherokee Office Enrollment Office at the above address will search its rolls for a fee.

Rolls and census records pertaining to Cherokees

1817–1835—Register of Cherokees Who Wished to Remain in the East, 1817–1819; Cherokee Emigration Rolls. Under the Treaty of 1817 at Turkey Town, the Cherokees ceded two large tracts of land and two small tracts of land east of the Mississippi River for one of equal area in the west between the Arkansas and White rivers. On 27 February 1819, another treaty was concluded with the Cherokee Nation in which the Cherokees ceded several other large tracts of land. The United States sought to extinguish title to certain Cherokee lands in the east by offering the Cherokees two options. One was for those who decided to remove to Arkansas; the other for those who did not wish to move. The latter could file for a reservation of 640 acres which would revert to the state upon the death or abandonment of the grantee. These reservations were in Alabama, Georgia, Tennessee and North Carolina. (See National Archives M208 or *Cherokee Reservees* by David Keith Hampton).

In a treaty concluded 6 May 1828, the Cherokees ceded their lands in what is now Arkansas for lands in what is now Oklahoma. Under this treaty the United States was to furnish the following items to each head of a Cherokee family then residing east of the Mississippi River who desired to remove: a good rifle, ammunition, a blanket, a brass kettle or beaver trap and five pounds of tobacco. They also were to be compensated for all improvements he/she abandoned. Additionally, the United States paid the expenses of removal and furnished subsistence for one year, and each head of family who took four persons with him received $50. Several hundred Cherokees emigrated from the east to the west under these provisions.

The emigration rolls resulting from the treaties of 1817–1819 and 1828 are in the records of the Bureau of Indian Affairs in the National Archives in Washington, D.C. However, apparently no emigration rolls were kept (or are extant) of those who emigrated prior to 1817.

These Cherokees later became known as the Old Settlers, Emigrant Cherokees or Western Cherokees. By 1835 the

Cherokees living west of the Mississippi River were estimated to be one-third of the tribe. The Cherokee Emigration Rolls, 1817–1835 contain the names of more than 1,600 heads of Cherokee families who signed up to immigrate to the West. Since no census was taken of the Old Settler Cherokees until 1851, these rolls provide the only list of those individuals prior to that date.

Not all of those who signed up to go actually went. There are separate muster rolls of those that did. The Cherokee Nation then covered certain parts of Alabama, Georgia, Tennessee and North Carolina. See *Cherokee Emigration Rolls, 1817–1835*, transcribed by Jack D. Baker.

☐ **1835 Census or Henderson Roll**—This is a census (covering the Cherokee Nation in Alabama, Georgia, North Carolina and Tennessee) that was taken before the general removal in 1838–9 on the Trail of Tears. It contains the names of heads of families, number of those who could read Cherokee and English, lists the number of (but not by name) full-bloods, half-bloods, quadroons and whites in each family, and the residence (state, county and watercourse). It also references those that were mixed-Catawbas, mixed-Spaniards, mixed-African Americans, reservees, and descendants of reservees. Available on microfilm and in print. The latter is entitled *Those Who Cried*, compiled by James W. Tyner.

☐ **1848 Census or Mullay Roll**—This is the first census of what would become known as the Eastern Band of Cherokees. It contains 1,517 entries. It was compiled to enroll those individuals and families who were in North Carolina at the time of the ratification of the Treaty of New Echota (23 May 1835) and who did not remove to the west. Arranged by county and township.

☐ **1851 Census or Siler Roll**—This is a census of the Cherokees living east of the Mississippi River (in North Carolina, southeastern Tennessee, Alabama and Georgia) who were eligible for a per capita payment authorized by Acts of Congress of 30 September 1850 and 27 February 1851. It is arranged by state and thereunder by county. It contains about 1,700 names. All names are related by family group, with the relationship column giving the relationship to the head of the family. In the "blood" column is noted either I (Indian) or W (white). There is an index to this roll. White persons who intermarried with Cherokees after 23 May 1836 were not included.

☐ **Old Settlers Roll, 1851**—This roll includes names (only) of all of the Old Settlers (those who emigrated prior to the forced removal in 1838/9) who were still living in 1851 in Cherokee Nation (northeastern Oklahoma) and their children—unless the mother was an Emigrant Cherokee (1838/9). If the mother was an Eastern Cherokee Emigrant, the children appear with her on the **Drennen Roll**. The **Old Settlers Roll** is arranged by Cherokee Nation district and thereunder by family group, often without a surname, or in the Cherokee form. This roll also includes 44 family groups that are listed as nonresidents.

☐ **1852 Chapman Roll**—This roll was used to make the per capita payments to the Eastern Cherokees (those then living east of the Mississippi River) based on the census take by Siler in 1851. These payments were made in December 1851 and January 1852. Arranged by enrollment number and thereunder by county and town. It contains name, age and relationship to head of household.

☐ **1852 Drennen Roll**—This is the first census of the Cherokees living in what is now northeastern Oklahoma, after the removal in 1838–9. It is arranged by Cherokee Nation district and thereunder by family group. It contains names of 14,094 individuals. Also, in an additional section, known as the *Disputed Roll*, are listed 102 family groups (273 persons) who immigrated to the west prior to the Treaty of New Echota (1835) but who returned to the east before the removal. This list was compiled as a receipt roll for a per capita payment of $92.83 made to the Cherokees living in the west who removed as a result of and after the Treaty of New Echota.

☐ **Tompkins Roll, 1867**—This is a census record of Cherokees residing in the Cherokee Nation (northeastern Oklahoma). Approximately 13,566 individuals are listed. It is inconsistently arranged. Most are arranged by Cherokee Nation district and family group, but the Delaware District lists adult males first, then minor males, and finally females. This roll includes the name (some only the Cherokee name), age, sex and an indication if the individual is white, half-breed or colored. The **Tompkins Roll Freedmen Indices, 1867** consists of two indices for this roll—available at Regional Branch of National Archives in Fort Worth. One is alphabetical by the first two letters of the surname; the other is alphabetical by the first two letters of given name. The indices give name, page number and district of residence of the Freedmen listed on this roll.

☐ **Swetland Roll of Eastern Cherokee, 1869**—This is the census record of the Eastern [Band of] Cherokees who appear on the **Mullay Roll** as remaining in North Carolina at the conclusion of the Treaty of 1835, or were the descendants of such persons as were enrolled by Mullay and were alive at that time. It is arranged by township, thereunder by family group. It gives name, Swetland Roll number, relationship to head of household, age, **Mullay Roll** number and a remarks column that sometimes includes an individual's relationship to a Mullay enrollee.

☐ **List of Rejected Claimants, 1878–80**—This is a list of persons who appeared before the Cherokee Commission on Citizenship and whose claims were rejected. It is arranged by type of decision and thereunder by case number—contains name of claimant and decision.

☐ **Cherokee Census, 1880**—This census was authorized to facilitate a per capita payment of $16.55 "for purchase of bread stuffs"—later referred to as bread money. It was taken in March 1880. Any Cherokee or *intermarried white* appearing on this census was not challenged by either the courts or the Dawes Commission as the Final Roll was prepared in 1902. The Dawes census cards note if a person appeared on this census, any variation in name, district and census number. There is an index to it, arranged by Cherokee Nation district and thereunder in roughly alphabetical order. Missing are all of schedule one and three for Cooweescoowee District. Schedule 1—is Cherokee citizens, including Native, Adopted White, Shawnees, Delawares and Freedmen. Schedule 2—Orphans; Schedule 3—Rejected claimants; Schedule 4—Individuals whose claims to citizenship were pending; Schedule 5—Intruders; and Schedule 6—Individuals living in the Cherokee Nation under permit.

☐ **Cherokee Citizenship Commission Docket Book, 1880–84**—It provides names of claimants, nature of claim and the decision of the commission. Arranged by session and thereunder by case number.

☐ **Hester Roll, 1884**—This is the roll of Eastern [Band of] Cherokees (those living east of the Mississippi River at the time) and those claiming to be Cherokee who were attached to the Qualla Reservation of extreme western North Carolina; it includes names of persons living in 13 states. It also includes an individual's **Hester Roll** number, **Chapman Roll** number, Indian name, English name, relationship to head of household, age, ancestor, latest spelling of name and residence. It is arranged by household, and has an index.

☐ **Cherokee Census Roll, 1886**; and **Cherokee Census and Receipt Rolls, 1890.** The 1886 roll covers the Cherokee Nation in northeastern Oklahoma by Cherokee district; was made from an 1886 per capita receipt roll of Cherokee Citizens by Blood. The 1890 census and receipt rolls are by Cherokee district and thereunder alphabetically by first letter of the surname. Includes individual's name, roll number, age, gender and whether citizen was a Native Cherokee, Adopted Delaware, Shawnee, White or Freedman. It also lists orphans under 16, rejected claimants, persons whose claims to citizenship were pending, intruders and persons living in the Cherokee Nation under permit. Additionally, this census roll contains information about improvements on farms, farm products, livestock, machinery, manufacturing, schools, missions and churches, miscellaneous (number of toll gates, pianos, bee stands, etc.), merchandise and minerals.

☐ **Cherokee Freedmen (Wallace) Roll, 1890–93**—This roll is a census taken in 1890 of those Cherokee Freedmen eligible to receive a per capita payment authorized in 1888. It was based on an 1883 census of Cherokee Freedmen. It includes a list of authenticated Freedmen who appear on the 1883 roll, individuals who died between 1883 and 1890, individuals admitted by Wallace and those classified as *Free Negroes.* It also contains a list of those whose rights were questioned by the Commissioner of Indian Affairs and supplemental lists of those who were admitted by the Secretary of the Interior. This roll was set aside as fraudulent by a decree 8 May 1895 of the United States Court of Claims and was never recognized by the Cherokee Nation. There is an index to it, arranged alphabetically by surname.

☐ **Cherokee Census Roll, 1896**—This is the first roll of residents of the Cherokee Nation, Indian Territory, to provide information about the blood degree of enrollees. It is arranged by Cherokee district and thereunder by roll number. There is an index, but it is not considered adequate for locating names. It includes name, roll number, age, sex, precinct (town), proportion of blood or nativity, and place of birth. Also includes: Adopted (white), orphan, asylum, rejected, colored, doubtful, Shawnee and Delaware citizens.

☐ **Old Settlers Payment Roll, 1896**—This roll was based on families living in the Cherokee Nation (northeastern

Oklahoma) in 1851. This payment resulted from a decision of the U.S. Court of Claims made 6 June 1893. This is a receipt roll for a per capita payment of $159.10. The first section is for those *Old Settlers* still living in 1896; this roll provides a cross-reference to the enrollee's family group on the **1851 Old Settler Roll,** card number, name, age, sex and post office address. The information on the deceased *Old Settlers* includes their name, a cross-reference to the **1851 Old Settlers Roll** for that person, card number, names and relationship of heirs receiving payment, along with their age, sex and post office address. There also is a section which includes the names of the *Old Settlers* who were not located in 1896.

☐ **The Final (Dawes) Roll of Citizens and Freedmen, 1902–6.** This roll serves as the only basis for determining eligibility for membership today in the Cherokee Nation of Oklahoma and for receiving benefits through that tribe. There were originally 32,926 entries for Cherokees, but some were stricken from the roll because of death, non-citizenship or as duplicate entries. In 1914, 127 more names were added. The Delaware Cherokees include 197 persons who were adopted into the Cherokee tribe. This roll is arranged by tribe and thereunder by enrollment category and thereunder in numerical order by roll number.

☐ **The Index to the Final (Dawes) Roll, 1902–6,** gives name and roll number. It is arranged by tribe and thereunder by enrollment category and thereunder in roughly alphabetical order by the first two letters of the surname. However, a surname may appear in several groupings.

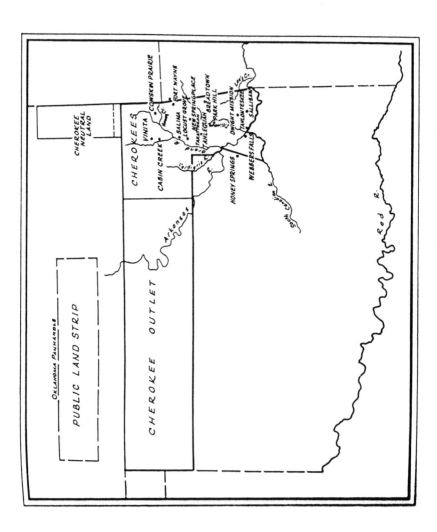

New home of the Cherokees, west of the Mississippi River.
From *The Cherokee*, by Grace Steele Woodward. Copyright (C) 1963 by the University of Oklahoma Press.

Select Bibliography

Listed here are many of the works that have been of use in the making of this book. It is by no means a complete record of all the works and sources I have consulted. Hopefully, this will serve as a convenience for those who wish to pursue additional genealogical and historical research pertaining to Cherokees.

Books

Ashton, Sharron Standifer. *1880 and 1890 Census, Canadian District, Cherokee Nation, Indiana Territory.* Oklahoma City, OK: Oklahoma Genealogical Society, 1978.

Awtrey, Hugh R. *New Echota: Birthplace of the American Indian Press.* Washington, D.C. Government Printing Office, 1941.

Baker, Jack D. *Cherokee Emigration Rolls 1817–1835.* Oklahoma City, OK: Baker Publishing, 1977.

_____, and David Keith Hampton, eds. *Old Cherokee Families: Notes of Dr. Emmet Starr.* Oklahoma City, OK: Baker Publishing Co., 1978 (Volumes One and Two).

Blankenship, Bob. *Dawes Roll "Plus" of Cherokee Nation, 1898.* Cherokee, NC: Cherokee Roots Publications, n.d.

_____. *Guion Miller Roll "Plus" of Eastern Cherokee, East & West of Mississippi, 1909.* Cherokee, NC: Cherokee Roots Publications, n.d.

Carseelowey, James Manford. *My Journal.* Tulsa, OK: Oklahoma Yesterday Publications, n.d., facsimile reprint of the original.

_____. *Indian Territory Notes.* Tulsa, OK: Oklahoma Yesterday Publications, 1980, facsimile reprint of the original.

_____. *Cherokee Notes.* Tulsa, OK: Oklahoma Yesterday Publications, n.d., facsimile reprint of the original.

_____. *Cherokee Pioneers.* Tulsa, OK: Oklahoma Yesterday Publications, n.d., facsimile reprint of the original.

_____. *Early Settlers.* Tulsa, OK: Oklahoma Yesterday Publications, n.d., facsimile reprint of the original.

_____. *Cherokee Old Timers.* Tulsa, OK: Oklahoma Yesterday Publications, n.d., facsimile reprint of the original.

Chase, Marybelle W., comp. *Index to Payment Roll for Old Settler Cherokees 1896.* n.p., 1989. [an index to the microfilm copy of the payment roll; NARA: T-985].

_____. transcriber. *Index to Civil War Service Records—Watie's Cherokee Regiments.* n.p., n.p., 1989. [an index to First and Second Cherokee Mounted Volunteers (Confederates) from NARS M258, rolls 79, 80 and 90].

Cherokee Connections

_____. *Records of the Cherokee Agency in Tennessee, 1801–1835.* Tulsa, OK: M. W. Chase, 1990.

Clark, Mary Whatley. *Chief Bowles and the Texas Cherokees.* Norman, OK: University of Oklahoma Press, 1971.

Conley, Robert J. *The Witch of Goingsnake and Other Stories.* Norman, OK: University of Oklahoma Press, 1988.

Corkran, David H. *The Cherokee Frontier: Conflict and Survival, 1740–62.* Norman, OK: University of Oklahoma Press, 1962.

Corn, James Franklin. *Red Clay and Rattlesnake Springs: A History of the Cherokee Indians of Bradley County, Tennessee.* Cleveland, TN: n.p., 1959.

Croom, Emily. *The Genealogist's Companion & Sourcebook.* Cincinnati, OH: Betterway Books, 1994.

Debo, Angie. *And Still the Waters Run: The Betrayal of the Five Civilized Tribes.* Norman, OK and London, England: University of Oklahoma Press. Reprint. Originally published Princeton, NJ: Princeton University Press. Paperback edition, fifth printing, 1989.

Douthat, James L. *Robert Armstrong's Survey Book of Cherokee Lands: Lands Granted from the Treaty of 27 February 1819.* Signal Mountain, TN. Institute of Historic Research, 1993.

Ehle, John. *Trail of Tears: The Rise and Fall of the Cherokee Nation.* New York: Doubleday, 1988.

Everett, Dianna. *The Texas Cherokees: A People Between Two Fires, 1819–1840.* Norman, OK: University of Oklahoma Press, 1990.

Foreman, Grant. *The Five Civilized Tribes.* Norman, OK: University of Oklahoma Press, 1934, sixth printing, 1977.

_____. Indian Removal: *The Emigration of the Five Civilized Tribes.* Norman, OK: University of Oklahoma Press, 1932, 1953 (new edition), 1972; seventh printing, 1976.

Hampton, David Keith, comp. *Cherokee Reservees.* Oklahoma City, OK: Baker Publishing Co., 1979.

_____. transcribed and edited. *Cherokee Old Settlers: The 1896 Old Settler Payroll and the 1851 Old Settler Payroll. n.p. 1993.*

Hill, Edward M. *Guide to Records in the National Archives of the United States Relating to American Indians.* Washington: NARS, 1981.

Hoskins, Shirley Coates. *Cherokee Property Valuations in Tennessee, 1836.* n.p.: Shirley Hoskins, 1984 (reproduction of handwritten documents).

Jordan, Jerry Wright, compiler. *Cherokee by Blood: Records of Eastern Cherokee Ancestry in the U.S. Court of Claims, 1906–1910.* 8 volumes. Bowie, MD: Heritage Books, Inc., 1988.

King, Duane H., ed. *The Cherokee Indian Nation: A Troubled History.* Knoxville, TN: University of Tennessee Press, 1979.

Kirkham, E. Kay. *Our Native Americans: Their Records of Genealogical Value.* 2 volumes. Logan, UT: Everton Publishers, Inc., 1980.

Cherokee Connections

McLoughlin, William G., *Cherokee Renascence in the New Republic.* Princeton, NJ: Princeton University Press, 1986.

_____, *Champions of the Cherokees: Evan and John B. Jones.* Princeton, NJ: Princeton University Press, 1990.

_____. *After the Trail of Tears: The Cherokees' Struggle for Sovereignty, 1839–1880.* Chapel Hill, NC: University of North Carolina Press, 1993.

Mauldin, Dorothy Tincup, ed. *Cherokee Advocate Newspaper Extracts* [May 1, 1845–March 3, 1906]. Tulsa, OK: Oklahoma Yesterday Publications, 1991. 7 volumes.

Mooney, Thomas G. *Exploring Your Cherokee Ancestry: A Basic Genealogical Research Guide.* Tahlequah, OK: Cherokee National Historical Society, 1987.

Morgan, Anne Hodges and Rennard Strickland, editors. *Oklahoma Memories.* Norman, OK: University of Oklahoma Press, 1981.

National Archives and Records Administration. *American Indians: A Select Catalog of National Archives Microfilm Publications.* Washington, DC, National Archives Trust Fund Board, 1984.

National Archives and Records Administration. *Guide to the National Archives of the United States*, Washington, DC: National Archives Trust Fund Board, 1987, reprint.

O'Donnell III, James H. *The Cherokees of North Carolina in the American Revolution.* Raleigh, NC: North Carolina State University Graphics, 1976.

Perrone, Bobette, H. Henrietta Stockel and Victoria Krueger. *Medicine Women, Curanderas, and Women Doctors.* Norman, OK: University of Oklahoma Press, 1989.

Purdue, Theda. *Nations Remembered: An Oral History of the Cherokees, Chickasaws, Choctaws, Creeks, and Seminoles in Oklahoma, 1865–1907.* Norman, OK, 1993 (paperback edition).

Shadburn, Don L. *Cherokee Planters in Georgia 1832–1838.* Pioneer-Cherokee Heritage Series Volume 2. Roswell, GA: W.H. Wolfe Associates, Historical Publications Division, 1989.

Sober, Nancy Hope. *The Intruders. The Illegal Residents of the Cherokee Nation 1866–1907.* Ponca City, OK: Cherokee Books, 1991.

Speck, Frank G., and Leonard Broom in collaboration with Will West Long. *Cherokee Dance and Drama.* Norman, OK: University of Oklahoma Press, 1983 (new edition), 1993 first paperback printing.

Starr, Emmet. *History of the Cherokee Indians and Their Legends and Folk Lore.* Muskogee, OK: Hoffman Printing Co., Inc., 1984. (Special Edition).

Stedman, Raymond William. *Shadows of the Indian: Stereotypes in American Culture.* Norman, OK: University of Oklahoma Press, 1982.

Strickland, Rennard. *The Indians in Oklahoma.* Norman, OK: University of Oklahoma Press, 1980.

Timmons, Boyce D. and Alice Tyner Timmon, editors. *Authenticated Rolls of 1880 Cherokee Nation—Indian Territory.* n.p. Chi-Ga-U, Inc., 1978.

Walton-Raji, Angela Y. *Black Indian Genealogy Research.* Bowie MD: Heritage Books, Inc., 1993.

West, C. W. "Dub." *Among the Cherokees: A Biographical History of the Cherokees Since Removal.* Muskogee, OK: Muskogee Publishing Company, 1981.

_____. *Legends and Folklore of the Cherokees.* Muskogee, OK: Muskogee Publishing Company, 1980.

Wilkins, Thurman. *Cherokee Tragedy: The Story of the Ridge Family and of the Decimation of a People.* New York, NY: MacMillan Company, 1970.

Woodward, Grace Steele. *The Cherokees.* Norman, OK: University of Oklahoma Press, 1963.

Articles

Carter, Kent. *Wantabees & Outalucks: Searching for Indian Ancestors in Federal Records.* Chronicles of Oklahoma. Vol. LXVI No. 1, Spring 1988, pp. 94–104.

_____. *Deciding Who Can Be Cherokee.* Chronicles of Oklahoma. Vol. LXIX, No. 2, Summer, 1991, pp. 174–205.

_____. *Federal Indian Policy: The Dawes Commission, 1887–1898.* Prologue. Vol. 22, No. 4, Winter, 1990, pp. 339–349.

Compact Disc

Objective Computing. *The Indian Question CD-ROM.* Objective Computing: Indianapolis, IN, 1994.

Selected Repositories

Cherokee National Historical Society
P.O. Box 515
Tahlequah, OK 74465

T. L. Ballenger Reading Room
John Vaugh Library
Northeastern State University
Tahlequah, OK 74464

Oklahoma Historical Society
Historical Building
2100 N. Lincoln Blvd.
Oklahoma City, OK 73105

Thomas Gilcrease Institute of American History and Art
1400 Gilcrease Museum Road
Tulsa, OK 74127

Cherokee Connections

Rudisill North Regional Library
Tulsa City-County Library
1520 N. Hartford
Tulsa, OK 74106

Museum of the Cherokee Indian
P.O. Box 1599
Cherokee, NC 28719

National Archives
7th and Pennsylvania
Washington, DC 20408

National Archives—Southwest Region
501 W. Felix, Bldg. #1
P.O. Box 6216 (mailing address)
Fort Worth, TX 76115

National Archives—Southeast Region
1557 St. Joseph Avenue
East Point, GA 30344

Georgia Dept. of Archives and History
330 Capitol Avenue, S.E.
Atlanta, GA 30334

Tennessee State Library and Archives
403 7th Avenue North
Nashville, TN 37219

Cherokee Publications Sources

Oklahoma Yesterday Publications
Dorothy Tincup Mauldin, publisher
8745 E. 9th St., Tulsa, OK 74112-4815
918/835-4118

Cherokee Research Publications
Marybelle W. Chase
5802 E. 22nd Place, Tulsa, OK 74114-2320
918/835-1031

Mary O'Brien Bookshop
2313 E. Admiral Blvd., Tulsa, OK 74110
918/587-9338

Cherokee Connections

Adair, county of, 25
Adairs, 19
Adams, John, 19
African Americans, 9, 27, 42
Alabama, 7, 21, 22, 23, 38, 39, 41, 42
Allen, Maud Bliss, 37
allotment, 27
Appalachians, 13, 17
applicants, rejected, 35
Arkansas, 20, 21, 22, 24, 26, 39, 41
Arkansas River, 20, 41

Baker, Jack D., 42
Baker Roll, 40
Bark Waterlizzard, 4
Bear, 14
Bear Meat, 39
Big Belly, 4
Bird, 14
Black Indians, 9
Blackburn, Rev. Gideon, 19
Blankenship, Bob, 10, 40
Blanket, 21
Blind Savannah, 14
blood revenge, 14
Blue, 14
Bowl, The, 20
Brave Eagle, 4
bread money, 44
British, 15, 17
Brown, Chief John, 24
    John, 39
Buchway, G. Eileen, 12

Cameron, Alexander, 17
Campbell, Arch, 39
Canadian, district of, 25
CDIB, 33
Chapman Roll, 43, 45
Cherokee
    census, 44, 45, 56
    citizenship commission, 45
    county of, 25
    missions, 38
    North Carolina, 40
    Phoenix, 21
    princess, 6

Cherokee (con't)
    reservees, 23, 42
    slave owners, 26
Cherokee Nation, districts of, 25
    of Oklahoma, 31, 33, 47
Chickasaw, 26, 39
Chief War Speaker, 15
Choctaw, 26, 39
Chunequateeskee, 4
Churchill, Frank C., 40
Civil War,
    Confederate, 39
    Union, 39
clan(s), 13, 14
citizenship, 27
Cleveland, Grover, 26
Compact of 1802, 19, 20
Cooweescoowee, district of, 25, 45
Court of Claims, 32
Craig, county of, 25
Creek, 26, 39
Creek Nation, 28
Curtis Act, 5

Dawes, Henry L., 27
Dawes Commission, 5, 26, 27, 28, 29, 30
Dawes Roll, 11, 47
Deas, Lt. Edward, 7, 8
Deer, 14
Deer Biter, 4
Delaware, 31, 47
    county of, 25
    district of, 25, 44
Delawares, 29, 30, 45 , 46
diseases, 16
Disputed Roll, 43
Doughertys, 19
Drennen Roll, 40, 43
Duwali, 21

earthquake, 20
Eastern Band
    of Cherokees, 39, 40, 42, 45
Eastern Cherokees, 24, 39
Emigrant Cherokees, 39, 41
English, 18

Cherokee Connections

ferries, 38
Fields,
    George, 39
    Turtle, 39
Flint, district of, 25
freedmen, 5, 9, 28, 45, 46

Galpins, 19
Georgia, 7, 20, 21, 22, 23, 39, 41, 42
Germans, 18
Goingsnake, district of, 25
government agents, 9
Great War Chief, 15
Guess, George, 39
Guion Miller, 32
Gunter, Chief Edward, 24

Hair Hanging Down, 14
Hampton, David Keith, 22, 41
Henderson Roll, 42
Hester Roll, 45
Holmes, Tony, 38
Hopewell, 17

Illinois, district of, 25
Illinois River, 24
Indian scouts, 39
Indian Territory, 8, 13, 28, 35, 37, 46
intermarriage, 9
intermarried,
    (Cherokees), 28, 29
    (whites), 43, 45
intruders, 25, 35, 46
Irish, 18
Iroquois, 13

Jackson, Andrew, 21
Jefferson, Thomas, 20
Jordan, Jerry Wright, 32

Keetoowahs, 37
Keowee River, 17

land cessions, 19
Little Flower, 4
Long Hair, 14
Looney, Chief John, 24
Louisiana, 21
Lowrey, Chief George, 24

marriage licenses, 38
Maryland, 33
Massachusetts, 27
matriarchal, 13
Mayes, county of, 25
McDonald, John, 17
McIntoshes, 19
McLoughlin, William G., 38
Mexico, 21
Mink, The, 39
missionaries, 9
Mississippi River, 20, 21, 41, 42, 43
Missouri, 20, 24, 39
mixed-bloods, 4, 8, 9, 11, 16, 18, 22, 32
Moravian Church, 37
Moravians, 19
Mullay Roll, 42, 44
Murchison, A. H., 38
Muskogee, county of, 25
    Oklahoma, 26, 28
muster rolls, 37

Nacogdoches, 21
National Archives, Fort Worth, 9
Nelson, Ken, 12
New Echota Treaty, 6, 8, 21, 40, 42, 43
New Orleans, 20
Night Hawks, 29, 37
Night Killer, 39
North Carolina, 7, 17, 21, 22, 23, 24,
    39, 40, 41, 42
Nowata, county of, 25

Ohio, 8
Oklahoma, 6, 13, 20, 22, 24, 25, 26,
    35, 37, 39, 41, 43, 44, 45, 47
Oklahoma Territory, 28, 38
Old Settlers, 21, 24, 39, 41, 42, 46
Old Settlers Roll, 43, 47
Oochgelogy, Georgia, 38
Osage, 39
Osage Nation, 24
Otter Lifter, 4

Paint, 14
Panther, 14
Parched Corn Flour, 39
permit records, 25, 26

Cherokee Connections

Plains Indians, 15
Pocahontas, 6
Powhatans, 6

Qualla Reservation, 40, 45

Raccoon, 14
Receipt Rolls, 1890, 45
red government, 15
Red River, 21
rejected claimants, 44, 46
reservations, 41
restricted Indians, 4
Rogers,
    Chief John, 24
    county of, 25
Ross, Chief John, 7, 8, 24
Ross's Landing, (Chattanooga), 7, 17
Rosses, 19
royalty, 16

Saline, district of, 25
Scots, 18
Scott, Gen. Winfield, 7
Seminole, 26, 39
Sequoyah, 19, 39
    county of, 25
    district of, 25
Shawnee, 45, 46
Siler Roll, 42
Skin Bayou, district of, 25
slave schedule, 1860, 26
slaves, 9
smallpox epidemic, 16
South Carolina, 15, 16, 17
Speaker, The, 39
Spencer, James, 39
Springplace, Georgia, 38
squatters, 25
Squirrel, The, 4
Stinking Fish, 4
Swetland Roll, 44
syllabary, 19

Tahchee, 21
Tahlequah,
    Cherokee Nation, 24

district of, 25
    Oklahoma, 34
Tahlonteskee, Cherokee Nation, 24
Takatoka, 21
teachers, 9
Tellico, Tennessee, 19
Tennessee, 7, 19, 21, 22, 23, 39, 41, 42
Tennessee River, 17
Texas, 21, 22
Thompson, Capt. John, 39
Tompkins Roll, 44
    Freedmen Indices, 44
traders, 9
Trail of Tears, 2, 6, 7, 9, 40, 42
Treaty of 1817, 22, 41
Treaty of 1819, 23
Treaty of Holston, 19
Trinity River, 21
Turkey Town, 41
Twister, The, 14
Tyner, James W., 42

U.S. Army, 8

Vann, Chief David, 24
Vanns, 19

Wallace Roll, (Freedmen), 46
Walton-Riji, Angela Y., 9
War Woman, 15
Washington,
    county of, 25
    George, 18
Wasosey, 39
Waterloo, Alabama, 7
Western Cherokees, 21, 24, 39
white government, 15
White River, 20, 41
White traders, 16(2)
Whiteley, Lt. R. H. K., 7
Wild Cat, 14
Wild Potato, 14
Wind, 14
Wolf, 14
Woodward, Grace Steele, 6
Wrinkle But, 4
Wrosetawastow, Chief, 16
Young Wolf, 39